Ordinary Income
Extraordinary Wealth

You Will Become Rich

BY DOMINIC J.FLEMING

CHAPTER 1

RICH UNCLE DOM

I got the name Rich Uncle Dom at a birthday party for one of my nephews. He is a typical kid, into Little League Baseball and computer games.

Recalling my own youth I gave him the perfect gift-cash. He opened the envelope and pulled out a one hundred dollar bill. Ben Franklin was always one of my favorite Americans.

His eyes grew wide. His jaw dropped. The envelope slipped to the floor. He just stared at that bill, looking at both sides over and over.

His brother asked, "Who's that from?"

"Rich Uncle Dom," he said.

"Yeah, he's a lawyer," his brother said.

Two things struck me at that time. The first that I was rich. Not necessarily in the psych- speech of a rich life with friends, family, and health, but in the concrete dollar and cents world of money in the bank, readily convertible assets worth well over seven figures.

The other conclusion was that the kids had it wrong. True I was a lawyer, but the law did not make me rich.

I began as a government lawyer and went on to practice criminal law representing people of middle and lower class incomes. I represented clients from the Public Defender's Office. I was often times paid less than the fry guy at McDonald's.

I thought about those things that made me rich. I listed the methods that worked for me and all the strategies that failed. I realized the path to my own financial wealth was like a mighty river fed from many small springs and tributaries, without which the river would not exist.

I also realized that many of these contributions to my wealth had no obvious connection to money or investing. I knew anyone, especially my young relatives, could apply the lessons I learned to create their own wealth. I also knew it would be a good idea to let them know about some of the mistakes I made so they could avoid making the same ones.

At family get-togethers I had told them about the time I climbed Mount Everest in my underwear or jumped out of an airplane without a parachute or walked barefoot in the snow to school, uphill both ways. They all knew Uncle Dom told stories. They also received letters from me. I usually told them about someone famous or not so famous with an interesting story to tell that shared the same first name with each of them.

If I talked to them, minimum credibility. If I wrote it on paper, perhaps incredible or even far fetched, but the absolute truth.

I want them and everyone else to become wealthy, to have enough money to pay attention to and enjoy the many other things life offers, without the constant worry of where the next dollar is coming from or how something important and necessary can be paid for.

Many people have the mistaken notion that financial wealth is only for the few, the lucky, or the gifted. Others think financial wealth is like a pie with only a few limited number of slices to go around.

The reality is just the opposite. The only luck involved is to be born in or live in a free society like the United States of America.

Learning the lessons of wealth accumulation coupled with a little effort will make you rich.

Financial wealth is more like bread baking than cooking pie. Your knowledge and effort is the flour and yeast you put in. The more in and left to properly rest the bigger the loaf. Even more importantly the more others put in, the bigger the loaf for all of us to share.

CHAPTER 2

BE THE PIPER

My father was a wonderful man. One of my early fond memories is of him tucking me into bed and telling me a story. He would not read to me. He would make up the stories.

My favorites were the dog stories. Looking back I now realize all the dog stories had the same plot. Dad would choose a particular breed of dog, describe it in detail and make the dog a hero who did something extraordinary like saving someone's life.

The Saint Bernard struggles through drifting snow to save the downed skier. The German Sheppard in one story braves enemy fire to save a soldier. In another he saves a police officer from bank robbers. The Dalmatian winds his way through the burning rubble of a collapsing building to save a fireman.

I believed all these stories to be true. Dad put detail into his stories that made them believable–names of the dogs and people, vivid descriptions of the places where the action took place, and the life threatening injuries suffered by the dogs who were the heroes of his stories.

My belief that everything my Dad said was true indirectly led me to discover the first secret that made me a millionaire.

One day he was talking to my mother (a truly remarkable lady), about what I have no idea, but I heard him say, "Everybody's got to pay the Piper sooner or later."

I had no idea what that meant or what a piper was, but what a great job I thought. A job where sooner or later everybody in the world had to pay you. And if everybody in the world had to pay you, you would surely make more than a hundred dollars, and a hundred dollars was surely enough to buy anything you would ever need.

I got a little older and started school. I learned the expression had more to do with "The Pied Piper of Hamelin" by Robert Browning or even a Scottish rite involving the poetry of Robert Burns and the consumption of whiskey and haggis on January 25 when Scotland celebrates the birth of that great poet. (Haggis is a sheep's stomach stuffed with oatmeal, suet, lamb's liver, onion, and spices–I guess whiskey would have to accompany it.) Despite my new knowledge I still thought it a great idea to be the Piper. If not everybody had to pay me, sooner or later, I could certainly pay myself. I earned some money. I became my own Piper and paid myself part of every dollar I earned.

In the beginning the amounts were trivial, a few pennies or a nickel out of the quarter I earned walking to the corner store for bread, milk, and lunch meat. I would give the money I saved to my Mom and ask her to save it for me. The rest I would spend on movies, comic books or baseball cards. (If I would have saved those comic books and base-ball cards I would be far, far richer than I actually am.)

As I matured and worked summer and part time jobs around my school schedule I made it a habit to always pay the Piper, and the Piper was me.

My payment goal to the Piper was a minimum of ten per-cent (10%) of what I earned, but if I could pay more I would.

When something becomes a habit it soon becomes auto-matic and painless. From each paycheck I received my first expense was to pay at least ten per cent to the Piper.

As a youngster this payment went to the Brehm's Building and Loan Association where I had a passbook account. In later years the check would go to deferred compensation, stocks, mutual funds, futures, currency spreads, joint ven-tures, SEPs, 401(k)s, real estate, IRAs, and a variety of other ventures, many of which failed miserably.

The Piper was always the first one who got paid. He got paid before the rent, groceries, or entertainment. Sometimes I had to skimp, but the Piper always got paid.

The first secret I learned on my journey to the million-aire's club was to be the Piper and always pay him first.

CHAPTER 3

TIME GROWS MONEY OR GETTING PAID FOR DOING NOTHING

When I was five years old I started kindergarten at Brehms Lane Public School. Unlike today, kindergarten was a place for recess, story telling, milk and cookies, and naps. No reading, arithmetic, or spelling.

At one point we were encouraged to open up a savings account at Brehms Building and Loan. Sine the accounts had to be opened jointly with at least one parent, this was probably a marketing ploy aimed at the parents.

Despite the motivations of the building and loan many of my classmates and me ended up with little books crediting us with a few dollars which had been given to us by our parents for just this purpose. We were told that our money was being lent to the association who was going to use it so people could buy homes and would pay us back whenever we wanted it with interest. Interest we were told was extra money we got because we allowed the institution to hold

9

onto the money. The longer they got to hold it, the more we would get paid.

I did not understand much of what the man said. I made sure my passbook was kept safe: I gave it my mother.

That summer the family went to Atlantic City New Jersey for vacation. After checking into the hotel we took the elevator down to the first floor. My mother was pregnant with my second sister, holding the older sister in one arm, and holding my younger brother's hand with the other. I was holding his other hand. The elevator opened. There was a pool in the lobby. My brother said, "I'm going swimming, Mommy." He pulled himself away from us and jumped into the pool.

My mother screamed. I said, "Don't worry, I'll save him," and jumped in after him. A lady in the pool hauled us to the side. As soon as we got home I was enrolled in swimming lessons. My brother was enrolled a year later when he was old enough.

I soon forgot about that little book and engaged myself in the more important pursuits of exploring every climbable tree in Herring Run Park, pick up baseball games and, at night, fifty scatter (a more "mature" version of hide and seek).

Years passed. I still paid the Piper by giving my mother the pennies and nickels I was saving from small allowances and gifts from relatives on Christmas and my birthday. Higher finance was debating with myself whether to buy a pack of baseball cards or the newest Superman comic.

A moral dilemma struck me and my family during the summer of my sixteenth year. Up to that time it was okay to enjoy the summer. Work permits were available to kids under sixteen, but unless it was a family business, not many jobs went to the under sixteen year olds.

At sixteen you were supposed to work. Summer vacation now meant summer job. Because of my Atlantic City Experience I was now certified by the Red Cross as a Senior Life Savior.

I applied for and was offered a number of jobs at area pools. All paid minimum wage except one. That pool was on the roof of an apartment building near Johns Hopkins University. The job paid twenty five cents more an hour than the other jobs and it was for a six day work week which meant one day of overtime.

The moral dilemma was that it required I worked the weekends, which meant Sunday, which meant I would miss Sunday mass. It was a sin to miss mass on Sunday. Back then the Saturday option was not available.

I was the oldest of six children and my mother worked. She was about the only woman in my neighborhood with a regular job. She was given pregnancy leave when no one even had a term for it. Of course, back then it was two weeks of unpaid leave.

When I brought this extraordinary dilemma to her attention, she looked at me for two whole seconds. "Take the job," she said.

The job title was misleading. The pool was tiny. It was situated on the roof next to a chimney for the building's incinerator. My principle duty was to skim the soot from the water so the elderly sun bathers had a pretty sight to view. A more accurate job description would have been janitor in a bathing suit.

Though the job was not the glamorous one I envisioned, the pay check was real. I was making an incredible amount of money. For every week I worked they gave me slightly more than one hundred dollars ($100.00). I was rich. The thought that I would get such a princely sum each week of the summer was incredulous.

I did not know what to do with the pay check. Mom reminded me of my account at Brehms. She found my pass book, gave it to me with a jar of money, mostly coins. It was all the money I had given her over the years to save for me.

The next night she brought home some coin wrappers. I wrapped the coins, pocketed a few bills (for paperback adventure novels now rather than comic books) and went to Brehms with my bag of money and my first paycheck.

The teller taught me how to fill out a deposit ticket. She saw my pass book and smiled. "We owe you a bunch of interest," she said.

She took my pass book to a machine that looked like an extra large typewriter. I wish I could tell you the machine went "Ka-Ching", but the sound it made was more like a dull thump. That dull thump sounded more times than I could count. It filled up my pass book, and another had to be placed in the machine.

I stared at the entries in my pass books. A true epiphany overcame me. I was being paid for doing absolutely nothing, and the longer I did absolutely nothing, the more I got paid.

My money was working for me twenty four seven, three hundred sixty five and a quarter days each and every year.

Time grew my money. In the ten plus years since the account was opened my money had almost doubled. My money made money. It did not need a supervisor, instructions, tools, an office, or anything. I was stunned. When I was watching TV, my money was working. When I was sleeping, my money was scurrying around, doing its thing and adding to my bottom line.

Memorize this lesson. Make it part of your life. Sure everyone knows about this, but those who use this lesson are the ones who are not worrying where their next Lexus is coming from.

CHAPTER 4

UGLY IS TOO EXPENSIVE

There are laws on the books that are supposed to prevent discrimination based on race, age, sex, and nationality. You might be surprised at how limited these protections are, how difficult they are to enforce, and how easy it is to circumvent them. Trust me on this.

There are no laws to prevent one of the most invidious and pervasive forms of discrimination that exists today. It is practiced by companies both large and small and those in between, and even by the government at all levels. That is the discrimination against people who are significantly overweight and/or unattractive.

This is wrong and unfair. Just because something is wrong and unfair does not make it any less real. The reality must be dealt with.

There is the example of the executive who had to fill a supervisor's position. The decision was between two candidates, both female. One had only a high school education, but had been promoted to a leadership position in a smaller company and was largely responsible for a six fold increase in sales in her area during a two year period.

The other candidate had no work experience, but graduated from a prestigious college with a business degree with honors. Who got the job?

The blonde with the big boobs.

It's an old joke, but sadly, one with a lot of truth.

It is imperative in this country to look as good as you can. We are bombarded with advertising that portrays the fit and the good looking as winners. This attitude carries over to those people who make the decisions concerning our jobs, our promotions, our very lives. This attitude might not be conscious, but it exists.

We can't do anything about our genes, but we are able to control what and how much we eat. We also control the form, duration, and type of physical activity we engage in. The same applies to our style of dress, hairstyle, makeup, and other external features that cause others to consciously or unconsciously make judgments about us. Sixteen piercings, fourteen visible tattoos, cut offs and a halter might help you get a job as a bartender, but it is doubtful you'll get past the first interview at a mutual fund, or investment firm.

I love to eat. My two favorite meals are my last one and the next one. I grew up being taught that if I even left one or two peas on my plate I was at least partially responsible for starving children in China and Africa.

Various experts have preached magic formulas to insure a perfect weight. Eat carbohydrates. Eat protein. Take my pill. Use this supplement. Drink this shake.

Most of us are aware of this basic fact of life: if more calories go in than out we gain weight; if more go out than in, we lose weight. (One small controlled study produced evidence indicating that a group on a carbohydrate restricted diet eating three hundred more calories per day than another group actually lost more weight).

Good news? Probably not. There's also a significant body of knowledge indicating that such a diet leads to heart disease, the number one killer of both men and women in this country.

Some fruits and vegetables have come under attack. Studies tell us to be aware of the glycemic index. Potatoes are to be avoided. Watermelon is on the "Do Not Eat" list.

A report or study probably exists telling us that everything is bad for us. We can't ignore science, but use your common sense. Eat everything. Vary your food choices and eat four vegetables and three fruits every day.

Keep active. Walk briskly thirty minutes each day and do nothing else and you'll keep your heart healthy. It's not even necessary to walk continuously. Ten minutes three times a day is sufficient.

The most effective exercise program is the one you will stick to. Studies tell us that the program most of us will stick to is one that we do at our own home first thing in the morning. Keep an exercise dairy or write in a journal what you have accomplished. Have a partner assist you. Even if you live alone have someone you can call every day and tell him that you've accomplished your work out. If there's no one to call send yourself an E-mail.

"Uncle Dom, are you telling us that running around playing, or going to a gym are secrets that will make us rich?"

"Absolutely. If you ignore your health in the pursuit of wealth you will be sure to lose both.

"I already told you that many of the secrets of wealth accumulation do not appear to have a direct connection to money. These secrets are the keys to the golden kingdom."

CHAPTER 5

THE GREATEST INVESTMENT
OF THEM ALL

I grew up in a middle class neighborhood of row houses. Every main intersection had a church or a bar on a corner. Just about all of my neighbors were like me. We were all first or second generation Americans. I was Irish. The neighborhood had Poles, Italians, Germans, and other immigrant families.

Most were Catholic so the families were large and the money had to be stretched. In those days a good job was at Bethlehem Steel, the GM plant, or the government.

One thing we were all brought up with was where are you going to college? Few of the parents had gone to college. Many had never graduated high school. Yet that entire generation instilled in all of us the requirement of going to and graduating from college. There was no discussion of whether to go to college or not. The only discussion was of where are you going to go.

During those years anyone who wanted to go to college could afford it provided you went to your State school and worked full time during the summer and part time during the school year.

Our parents knew one thing that many seem to have forgotten. The American Dream is truly here for anyone who wants it. Our parents saw depression and soup lines, a global war, recession, factory closings and layoffs. But they knew the American Dream was there for their kids who went to college and worked for it.

Today the division between the haves and the have nots is more obvious. McMansions sprout up all through suburbia, while the neglect and decay of our inner cities is obvious to anyone who has the courage to drive through them.

A great number of our citizens remain in the self fulfilling prophecy of poverty, ignorance, and criminality. There's nothing wrong about being the fry guy at Burger King, but as a stepping stone only. This kind of job will not thrust you into Middle America with two cars, a big screen, and nice vacations.

Education was my greatest investment. It is still a fantastic investment. Today freshmen entering the top schools pay just about the same as those entering the non-ivy league. The reason– endowments.

Harvard, Yale, Stanford, and other top notch schools have so much money that once you get in tuition will be paid for. The Ivy League claims it does not offer athletic scholarships. Be an All-State lacrosse player with a low B average and apply to Brown University. Send me an invitation to your graduation party because you're sure to get in.

Where you graduate may have some influence on your first job, but after that your future is up to you.

Unfortunately, without that degree too many doors close on you. You can make a ton of money in your own plumbing, construction, or other business without a degree, but the acumen necessary to start and run such a business is much more than the ability to do the job itself.

The greatest failure of my generation was the inability to keep the cost of a college education affordable to anyone who chose to obtain one. Yet college is still attainable.

Going to a community college part time while working full time may be the only option available to you at this time of your life. Make the commitment and the investment. Your return on investment will be huge.

If you choose to enter a college in another state, take the steps necessary to become a resident of that state before you enroll. Establish residency. Emancipate yourself. Have your parents stop taking you as a deduction on their tax return. Change your address. Get a local driver's license. Register to vote. The process takes a year in most states, but the savings in tuition payments will be enough for a substantial down payment on a home.

Even after you acquire a degree your education must continue. You may need the sheepskin to enter the ranks of the middle class, but you'll also need to continue learning while making the jump from Middle America to rich.

The information age requires us to increase our knowledge on a daily basis.

"Uncle Dom, are you saying only a person with a college degree can get rich in this country?"

"No, but the journey to riches is easier and shorter with knowledge. On average the person with the college degree will earn greater than one million dollars more in a lifetime than the person without one. A million dollars may not be what it once was, but it still buys quite a few boxes of Fruit Loops."

CHAPTER 6

READING

In the information age the accumulation and dissemination of information is what earns profits and higher pay.

The most efficient and simplest method of information accumulation is by reading. I have more than twenty years of formal education and have read more than two thousand books, but the information I am about to impart was not taught in any course I took. I had to find this on my own.

I spent less time than most of my classmates studying for tests, yet I continued to get better grades than most of them. When I tried to share my methods, most chose not to follow through because in the beginning the process takes a bit more time than regular passive reading. After a short period of time you'll find your reading rate will rapidly increase, and, most importantly, your comprehension will improve tremendously.

To succeed in life you need to internalize information from many sources. This is the method I used to excel in school, work, business, and investing.

Passive Reading

I take much pleasure from passive reading. Novels have taken me around the world, tracked serial killers with great detectives, flown me through space to other civilizations and solar systems, and to all historical eras since the inception of civilization.

Passive reading is enjoyable and you should enjoy such a past time as much as you can.

Active Reading

Active reading is not the opposite of passive reading, but it is a different type of reading. You read passively for entertainment and enjoyment. You read actively for a definite purpose- to gain information, to learn how to do or accomplish something, to make more money, to get a better job, to become happier, to reduce stress, to live or love better, to bake a better cheesecake. In short, active reading is goal oriented. You wish to accomplish a particularized and definite goal.

This system of active reading is easy to learn, but it will require some effort and I've found from experience that most people will abandon the system and continue to rely on passive reading.

Focus

The first step seems a bit new age or metaphysical, yet it is very important to begin active reading this way.

Close your eyes and take three to five deep breaths. Focus on what you intend to get out of what you are about to read. Think about what you hope to accomplish by reading the material. Ask yourself these two questions: What information do I hope to learn? How will I benefit from that information?

Preview

Next quickly preview the entire content of your reading material. Glance at captions, bold face type, tables of contents, lists, and other materials the author has accented for you.

Next run your fingers over the words from start to finish without pause. Follow your finger. You will not be reading much at first but you will be training your brain to read faster, comprehend more, and not re-read what your eyes have already read once.

Read

Now read the material. When you first begin to read this way take a plain file card or piece of paper and cover what you've read. After a few weeks use your finger or other pointer to guide you through the material. Concentrate on getting your finger to move across the page at ever faster rates.

Soon you will be reading at over five hundred words a minute and your potential rate can exceed a thousand words a minute.

Review

This is the most important aspect of comprehension.

Repetition causes remembrance.

Repetition causes remembrance.

Repetition causes remembrance.

Review what you have read. Ask if you've obtained the information you desired. Repeat the basic information to yourself in outline form focusing on key words or phrases that sum up the ideas of the material.

Plan

Your active reading plan should be to spend about one half hour with the material. As your reading rate increases and your comprehension levels improve the number of pages read using active reading will increase significantly.

At each session plan on active reading for only one half hour at a time. If you need more time break the material down into one half hour increments and go through the process as detailed. Focus. Preview. Read. Review. Focus. Preview. Read. Review.

After a half hour session, spend a few minutes relaxing. It is not unusual for our attention to wander after that period of time. After all just about all of us were brought up on half hour TV shows.

After the two to four minutes of relaxation go to the next half hour and focus, preview, read, and review.

"Uncle Dom, if we learn to read your way, will you tell us anything about making all the money we need to be rich?"

"OK.

"The next lesson is very simple. The power of this concept is incredible."

CHAPTER 7

YOU CAN'T AFFORD THE
SECOND TOASTER

Many years ago I was in a department store with my mother. This was unusual. My Mom worked full time, I was one of six kids, and shopping was a chore for her, not an enjoyable past time.

I overheard a couple talking about buying a toaster. It was a nice looking toaster, fancier than our basic two slicer. She said they couldn't afford it. He said they needed it and might as well go first class. She insisted it was too expensive and they shouldn't waste the money. He said they could put it on their credit card. She agreed. They bought this twelve dollar toaster.

Some time later I asked my Dad if he had a credit card and what was it for. He said it was something to be used only in a dire emergency.

I asked him about the twelve dollar toaster. He told me those people were crazy and needed their heads examined.

I was skeptical (at the time I didn't even know what that word meant), but I knew arguing the point with Dad was a wasted effort. I believed a credit card was a pretty nifty thing. If you couldn't afford something you wanted you could put it on a credit card and take the thing home with you.

I guess my Dad knew he hadn't convinced me because a few days later he asked me how much the twelve dollar toaster actually cost when it was put on the credit card.

I knew Dad was a smart guy, but this was the dumbest question I ever heard. A twelve dollar toaster costs twelve dollars. No more. No less.

He showed me a chart he made up. At the time the prime interest rate was over ten per cent and the annual percentage rate on most credit cards was twenty two percent.

He explained the concept of credit and a credit card. He said that technically an item would be paid off before ten or twenty years went by, but convinced me that people who would use a credit card for a toaster would use it often for ordinary purchases, rather than in a dire emergency.

The chart looked something like this:

1.   12   + 2.64
2.   14.64   + 3.2208
3.   17.8608 + 3.929376
4.   21.7901 + 4.794
5.   26.584   + 5.848
6.   32.433   + 7.135
7.   39.569   + 8.705
8.   48.274   + 10.62
9.   58.89   + 12.957
10. 71.851   + 15.807
11. 87.658   + 19.284

12. 106.943 + 23.527
13. 130.470 + 28.703
14. 159.174 + 35.018
15. 194.192 + 42.722
16. 236.915 + 52.121
17. 289.036 + 63.588
18. 352.624 + 77.577
19. 430.201 + 94.644
20. 524.845 + 115.466 = $640.31

I was amazed. The explanation made sense. The numbers seemed true. So I concluded the twelve dollar toaster actually cost over six hundred dollars. Wrong again. Dad wasn't through.

"What happens if we take that twelve dollars, put it in the bank and get paid the same amount the credit card company gets?" he asked.

Since the number $640.31 was right in front of me that's what I said.

"So you see that twelve dollar toaster put on a credit card actually ended up costing you $1280.62," he said.

"What's the point, Uncle Dom? No toast at your house?"

"The secret is never, never, ever pay interest for any thing except your home, your education, your business, or something that will increase in value."

CHAPTER 8

TWO PURCHASES

Two large purchases we make sooner or later are for housing and transportation. We need a place to live and the days of life without an automobile are long gone.

Housing

Owning a home has always been part of the American Dream. As you drive along suburbia you'll see McMansions on either side of the road: four thousand square feet or more of living space on a small lot. This is not middle class living. It's merely an obvious example of the expanding gap between the rich and the poor, or it's an example of someone who is house poor.

Your goal should be to be on the rich side of the economic gap, but not house poor.

Avoid renting. Our government subsidizes home ownership by allowing deductions for mortgage interest. Few other non business deductions are so lucrative.

Buying a home to live in and following some simple rules puts you on the path to being rich. For most people their home becomes their biggest asset. In times of economic slumps, the person with an affordable home still has a place to live. In times of economic booms his asset continues to increase in value.

The realtor's mantra of location, location, location has to become yours as well. You must focus on the neighborhood you are going to live in. Be sure it is one you can afford. Spend no more than two and one half to three times your gross earnings. Even better is to be in a home that only costs that factor of your net. (Gross and net here mean before or after taxes.)

Many factors go into your decision as to the neighborhood you are going to invest in. Schools, transportation, distance from work, community amenities are all important considerations. One friend refuses to live west of where he works believing the commute to and from work with the sun in his eyes is not worth it.

Once you decide on an affordable neighborhood it is imperative to look at every house on the market. Even if you need a friend, spouse, or relative to divide the houses you are looking at, be sure a visit is paid to every one. You will be amazed at the difference in value between similar houses. My second house was in move in condition and the asking price was a full forty percent less than a comparable house that would have needed to be gutted and fully rebuilt that was two blocks away.

A simple rule to follow would be to buy the cheapest house in the neighborhood. Cheapest here does not mean simply the one with the lowest asking price. It means the one that gives you the greatest value for the price.

Once you decide on the home you want to live in and know it is affordable avoid complicated financing arrangements. Put ten to twenty percent down and get the lowest fixed mortgage available with no pre payment penalty. Resolve not to re-finance for reasons other than a decrease in interest rates and further resolve to make an extra two or three payments a year toward the principle. Your goal is to pay off the mortgage. Living without a mortgage has you zooming down the path to becoming rich.

<u>Wheels</u>

The automobile is the second largest purchase most people make. The availability and variety of personally owned transportation is incredible. Travel main roads that are part of our highway system and try to count the numbers. Get off the highway and count the automobile dealer lots for new and used cars. Amazing.

Advertisers seldom sell transportation. You are being sold life style, luxury, safety, and ego enhancement.

The personal automobile changed America's landscape. It created suburbia and sprawl. It has become a necessity for most people rather than a luxury.

For years I could not afford a car of my own. Like most kids I yearned for a fast sports car. A corvette would be great, but an Aston Martin like James Bond's would be even neater.

The first car I purchased on my own was an eight year old Plymouth Duster. The paint had faded, the doors squeaked whenever they were opened or closed, oil had to be added regularly. The driver's seat was duck taped.

I knew nothing about cars. (Still don't), but I was religious about scheduled maintenance.

I calculated that I needed that Duster for at least eighteen months before I could save enough money to get a better car. That Duster provided me with mostly reliable transportation for over seven years. Even a car payment of only one hundred dollars a month would have created a wealth difference of over twenty thousand dollars. (Eight thousand four hundred on the debit side versus eight thousand four hundred invested on the credit side.) I know car payments do not run for seven years, and you need to factor in the cash cost of the automobile, but the average person accustomed to making car payments feels the need to buy another car once the payments end. This is a real wealth buster.

An automobile loses twenty percent or more of its value the day it is driven off the new car lot. Obviously, in most cases a used car is a better investment than a new one.

There is only one absolute rule for the purchase of a personal automobile. Buy any car you want as long as you pay cash for it. Never finance it. Never lease it. The rule is less than absolute if you own a business and the vehicle is to be owned or used by the business or if the business you work for provides some or all of the costs of the vehicle.

You cannot afford a second toaster. A financed automobile is financial sepuku. (Harakiri, ritualistic suicide done for honor or to atone for dishonor.)

"Uncle Dom, does this mean you're not going to buy me that two seater sports car when I'm sixteen?"

"Trust me, nephew. When you're sixteen get an old four door with a big back seat."

CHAPTER 9

FALLACIES

Picking sound investments involves the accumulation of information and knowledge. There is more information bombarding us than at any other time in history. The internet is a wonderful resource. It is also the prime purveyor of misinformation and falsehood.

Applying logic to information accumulation helped me tremendously in making many right moves in my investments.

I was surprised how a college philosophy course helped me so much in amassing wealth. The course was logic.

The course started with the most famous of all syllogisms:

All men are mortal.
Socrates is a man.
Socrates is mortal.

A syllogism is a formal argument consisting of a major and minor premise with a conclusion derived from the premises.

The information from the course that helped me the most in acquiring a fortune were the chapters on fallacies.

A fallacy is simply a statement or argument based on a false or invalid inference.

The fallacy I should have paid more attention to was the authority fallacy.

When I first invested in an area other than simply putting the money in a bank or savings or loan I had only a small amount to invest. Although the amount was small in every measurable sense of the word, the money was mine and I did not want to see it disappear. I poured over books and periodicals and taught myself how to read financial pages and a balance sheet, and learned basic accounting principles and procedures.

A few years passed and my meager sums grew into an amount that got noticed by the broker assigned to my account. Rather than continue along my own path, I allowed him to make many financial decisions concerning the stocks I bought and sold.

I should have better internalized that philosophy course and put into practice the authority fallacy.

Just because an argument or an opinion comes from an authority or an expert does not make a claim valid. You must look to the underlying basis of the argument or claim to see if it makes sense.

Worded very indelicately: Opinions are like assholes. Everyone has one and most of them stink.

I allowed a person "in the business" to make investment decisions I did not fully comprehend or agree with. My thinking was that if you hire a professional you should take their advice. Luckily, I did not let him make all the decisions.

Knowledge of another fallacy, "get on the band wagon", saved me a tremendous amount of money.

At one point every one I knew was investing in one "dot. com" business or another. They claimed to be doubling and tripling their money in very short periods of time.

I studied some of the companies. It made no sense to me. Some of these companies did not have a single dollar in sales, much less any profit or earnings.

On paper they were worth hundreds of millions of dollars.

I truly thought I was missing a great opportunity and I continued looking for a "dot.com" that I felt comfortable investing in. Thankfully I never did.

Another fallacy that aided my financial growth was "correlation is not causation." An example would be:

More men than women watch football on television.

More men than women are in prison for committing violent crimes.

Therefore, watching football on television causes men to commit violent crimes.

Being aware of that fallacy along with the related "Post hoc ergo propter hoc" fallacy have added quite a bit to my finances. This fancy Latin expression simply means "after the fact, because of the fact." Just because one thing precedes another does not mean the first caused the second. The crow of the rooster does not cause the sun to rise in the sky.

Financial analysts employ charts and graphs in an attempt to predict the price or direction of a stock, fund, or segment of the economy. Knowledge of these fallacies cause me to look for reasons a price may rise rather than looking at a graph that points in that direction.

Examine things closely to see if there is a logical connection between the two things. A simple example:

The Federal Reserve announces an increase in the Prime Rate.

Stock prices decline.

We know that just because one thing occurs after another does not mean that there is a necessary causation between the two.

Consider logical reasons for any connection. In the example a hike in the Prime Rate means that bond issuers will have to increase the interest rate payable on their bonds to attract buyers. This may mean that investment money flows from stocks to bonds and hence stock prices decline because investors are selling the stocks in order to have the money to buy the bonds.

Be aware that something happening second in time does not mean it was caused by its precedent. Look for the reasons why something has occurred.

The "General-Specific" and the "Specific-General" fallacies are self defining. A specific circumstance cannot be used to conclude that such an outcome will always occur. The converse fallacy is that even if a general rule is accurate does not guarantee that the circumstance you are examining will follow that general rule.

Mathematically the "General-Specific" puts your conclusion on a more secure footing than the "Specific-General." As a general rule a college graduate makes more money than someone without a degree. Between two people of similar race, age, sex, and background, you know one has a degree and the other has a high school diploma, you conclude that the one with more money is the one with the degree. Your conclusion may be correct, but if you are using such a conclusion to make an important decision in your life, get more information.

Let's say in the above example you acquire more information. You find out the one with more money dropped out of college to co-found a business. The business was Microsoft and the co-founder is Bill Gates. The general rule may be sound but act on it only after you accumulate enough information to see if it applies to your situation.

Sometimes you must act on less than complete information. Your overall body of knowledge can aid tremendously in filing in the gaps.

Years ago I was looking at a possible investment in Mattel, the toy company. I got the idea to look at the company even though it did not meet my general criteria of low cap value, from an article about the baby boomers waiting later in life to start families. The article predicted a boomlet because the boomers were now starting these families.

I assumed these kids would be getting toys and Mattel was a company I knew had something to do with the toy industry. I took a look at its financials. At the time I was not impressed.

Later I was talking with some of my contemporaries about the different toys and games available to kids that did not exist when we were young. One mother mentioned that despite all the new fangled stuff on the market her daughter's favorite toy was "Barbie." The other mothers chimed in about "Barbie" being a favorite of their daughters too.

I looked at Mattel's numbers again, but still did not like what I saw.

Later I read a financial article about Mattel that was very negative. If you believed the article the company was going into the toilet. Mattel was making a last ditch effort by ditching their computer games division.

I bought the stock.

If you question the logic of this decision, you are learning. A lot of my information was based on the "Specific-General" fallacy. The daughters of some people I knew liked "Barbie." I was hoping boomers would be buying a whole bunch of "Barbie" for the boomlet daughters.

The Mattel news was bad, but the numbers actually looked better. Which brings us to another kernel of financial wisdom: "Bad news been berry berry good for me too."

CHAPTER 10

BAD NEWS GOOD NEWS

In the financial world people almost always overreact to good or bad news. Once the news gets known to the average guy like me the market has probably done whatever it's going to do.

If the news is bad about a company or a sector of the economy its value had been battered by the time you become aware of it. Conversely if you see a headline proclaiming the next Microsoft that company's share price is likely to be at its all time high for a significant period of time.

My investment experience has taught me to pay little attention to good news, but to be very aware of the bad news.

Years ago (December 3, 1984) there was a disaster in Bhopal, India involving a gas leak at a power plant owned by a company primarily owned by an American company, Union Carbide.

Nearly four thousand people were killed and thousands suffered injuries ranging from minor to permanent impairment. Indian and American lawyers swarmed Bhopal signing up clients. Damages were estimated to be in the billions and the news was that Union Carbide would be bankrupted.

Before the disaster the stock price was around fifty dollars per share. After the disaster the price fell to the mid thirties.

The news subsequently revealed that the gas leak was caused by sabotage and not through negligence or a breakdown of machinery.

I bought the stock.

In 1986 the stock split three to one which meant that for every share owned before the split there were now three owned.

In the late nineties it became part of the Dow Chemical Company and was bought by Dow for over fifty dollars per share (or a profit of $120.00 for each and every share originally purchased). During this entire period the company paid dividends, meaning even more money came rolling in.

To happily complicate matters even further, part of Union Carbide, Industrial Gases, separated into a new corporation in 1992, Praxair, Inc. Buying into this company brought further growth.

Bad news available to the whole world can be used profitably by anyone, but seldom is.

In early 2004 I began to examine the Eastman Kodak Company as a possible investment. It was relatively inexpensive, a good value stock.

I did not buy it. The company did not seem to be focusing on the future of photography. Digital photography was taking over the market and Kodak had no significant presence in that market.

A short time later the company was taken off the Dow Jones Industrial list, one of the worst kinds of bad news.

A one year investment in Kodak at that time would have seen the stock price rise by 34% and paid a dividend of 25 cents per share on two occasions.

Two other companies were taken off the list the same time as Kodak, AT&T and International Paper.

A one year investment in AT&T would have risen 24% plus dividends totaling $1.20 per share. A sweet investment.

A one year investment in International Paper would not have been as profitable. The company's share price declined by about 7%. The company did pay dividends of $1.00 per share over the year.

An equal investment in all three companies would have returned 20% plus all those dividends.

Let's look at the investor who follows the good news. In April of 2004 three companies were added to the Dow Jones Industrial List: AIG, Verizon, and Pfizer.

The good news investor "knows" that when stocks are added to the list more institutions like mutual funds would be buying them and the price will go up. A no brainer investment.

A one year investment in AIG, a big company in the property and casualty insurance industry would have paid a nice dividend of $3.50 per share, but its adjusted share price declined 29%. You would have lost almost a third of your investment.

Verizon, a domestic telecom service industry, used to be part of Ma Bell, AT&T.

A one year investment would have netted $1.54 in dividends. It too declined in value. It dropped about 4%.

Pfizer is a major manufacturer of drugs. The baby boomers are getting older, taking more drugs. The company's been added to the Dow. What a great investment.

One year later you would have collected 70 cents in dividends, but seen your investment drop 25%.

An equal investment in these three companies would have declined about 20%.

So the real one year difference between the bad news investor and the good news investor in this example is a whopping 40% in favor of the person who goes against the grain.

Bad news can be berry, berry good for you too.

"Uncle Dom, where's the logic in bad news is good news and good news is bad news?"

The logic is sound. The herd mentality in going with the flow is obviously going to put you in the average percentile in whatever we're talking about. To go beyond average we must get away from the herd.

In October and November of 2008 the sub prime mortgage debacle led the investment community in a downward spiral that some pundits were comparing to the great depression.

My own portfolio decreased by almost thirty percent. The government bailed out many corporations and financial institutions. Home values dropped by forty percent.

For Uncle Dom this was the greatest buying opportunity to have come about in my adult life time. I worked hard and studied more companies. I bought, bought, bought. I did not know where these investments would be in three to four years, but I was willing to bet the ranch that the folks making the biggest mistakes of their financial lives were the ones selling. Buy on bad news.

CHAPTER 11

MY STOCK PICKING GUIDE

It would not be very informative to go through my thinking process about the usual stocks I bought which grew significantly. Most of these companies were bought or merged into larger companies.

Many of my picks were home runs and like most home run hitters I had a lot of strike outs. These investments went south and these companies went the way of the dodo bird.

The system I developed was comfortable for me as I looked for bargains. Bargain buying might not be as profitable as other methods for stock purchases, but for me I assumed the method was safer than other methods.

My mathematical system for identifying stocks of companies I wished to examine for possible purchase is simple in the explaining, but a little complicated in the doing.

I used a publication "Media General Financial Weekly" to get stock financial information and the Enoch Pratt Free Library to further delve into information about the company. Then I used the internet. The internet has now made the process much faster and more efficient. I primarily use "Yahoo Finance" and EDGAR, which will be explained later.

Small Company

Market capitalization is determined by the number of outstanding shares of stock multiplied by the current price of one share of the stock. A company with one million shares outstanding each worth ten dollars ($10.00) a share has a market capitalization of $10 million. The price drops a buck to nine dollars ($9.00), market capitalization drops to $9 million.

I looked for small companies having a market capitalization of $100 million to $900 million. On the internet the automatic range set is usually $150 million to $1 billion.

Industry

Comparing stocks or companies of different industries is a bit like comparing apples and rutabagas. You can do it. It may even be entertaining and worthwhile, but I found it was much more profitable to compare companies within the same industry.

The industry I examined would depend on all the things I read around the time that I was doing the examination. The financial newspapers and magazines are an obvious source, but a greater profit is often gleaned from knowledge outside the business pages. My investigation of Mattel was prompted by an article that talked of a baby boomlet as boomers were having children later in life than their parents, and conversations with mothers of little girls who said that "Barbie" was still the main toy the girls wanted. It did not fit my usual profile as its market capitalization was greater than $1 billion, but I bought the stock.

Bad news is always a key to finding great investments as I just outlined. If the cover of "Business Week", "Times", or "Forbes" has a cover story on some industry they say is doing a quick backstroke down the toilet, that is an industry to look at for a potential great investment.

Price Earnings Ratio

The price earnings ratio or P/E is a number found in every newspapers' financial pages or web sites where stocks are listed.

The number is the ratio (think fraction) of the price of the company divided by the company's earnings (what it makes). It is expressed on a per share basis.

Therefore P/E = Market value per share divided by Earnings per share (EPS).

The numbers listed are usually trailing P/E meaning a figure based on actual earnings from the last four business quarters or year.

The figure might be projected meaning what is expected in the next four quarters.

I use only trailing P/E as it is based on actual earnings and not on projections. No matter how technologically advanced the crystal ball becomes that is being used for these projected figures, I use actual earnings.

I looked at stocks with low P/Es. It is important to compare the P/Es within a single industry. The reason is simple. A low P/E in the gaming industry might be a high P/E in the transportation industry.

You may have heard of the "Dogs of the Dow" a stock picking system that emphasized the purchase of a Stock on the Dow Jones Industrial list with higher dividend yields.

(Dividend yield is the Annual Dividend Per Share divided by the Price Per Share). Higher dividend yields almost always means a lower P/E ratio.

It was a system of value investing so it was something that appealed to me, but since the Dow list is made up of stocks in many different industries it was not for me. I do look at the "Dogs" to give me an insight into a possible industry that might be out of favor.

I always looked at the average P/E ratio of the overall industry to compare with the individual company's P/E ratio.

Industry

There are many different industries that make up the American economy. Many companies are involved in more than one business or industry. For comparison purposes I always look at those companies that are more or less in the same industry.

Investment sources divide the economy into sectors such as consumer goods, basic materials, and financial services. Each sector is divided into industries. For example consumer goods is divided into at least thirty industries including appliances, auto parts, electronic equipment, and toys and games. There are over two hundred industries studied in these sources.

Which industry to look at? By now you should be able to guess. My initial examination for an investment would be in an industry that is not doing so well. If high oil prices are in the news I would look at stocks in industries adversely affected by high energy costs such as the automobile industry.

Once a specific industry is chosen for further study I would look at the average P/E of that industry over the preceding five years. I examined the last five years because that was the information I could access much easier than a greater period of time. The internet search of greater than five years is also more time consuming. If the current average P/E of the industry was lower than its five year average that was an industry deserving further study. **If the current average P/E of the industry was lower than its five year average that was an industry deserving further study.**

This led me to the general conclusion that here was an industry that was temporarily out of favor and in time would bounce back to at least average.

The next step was to look at the P/Es of the specific companies in the specific industry. I would focus on the companies with the lower current P/Es.

Next I would examine the P/Es of each of these companies over the last five years. My goal was to find the lowest P/Es relative to their five year averages. If the company had a higher five year P/E average than its current P/E that was a company to examine as a possible investment. Lower current P/E as compared to the company's five year average P/E was key to my investment strategy.

My thinking was simple. Look for small companies that were temporarily below average in industries that were temporarily below average. Once average and usual come back into place I would have made a very nice gain.

The final step was to find out as much as I could about the company. My investing began before the information explosion of the internet so the process of finding particular companies and information about these small companies was a bit time consuming, but fascinating.

To me it was like a miner searching for gold. My tools were provided at no charge from The Enoch Pratt Free Library, the public library of Baltimore, Maryland.

I wanted to know the major stockholders of the company, what the officers' experience and education were, what contracts existed, what future projects were in the works, what the balance sheet looked like, who had stock options that would pay off if the companies' stock price went above its present price, what patents and trademarks did the company own, if any law suits were pending. In other words I wanted to know everything there was to know about the company.

Most of these companies were relatively small and did most of their business in a single local area. I would use the library to check the area's local newspaper to find any news item concerning that company.

More often than not, I would have to write a company for its latest balance sheets. A lot of information can be learned by looking at the numbers and it was not difficult learning how to read one. (See "Balance Sheets for English Lit. Majors").

That is the system of stock picking that helped make me a millionaire. Small companies with a P/E lower than its five year average in an industry with a P/E lower than its five year average.

It is simple to summarize. With the internet, finding the companies for further study as possible investments is less time consuming than ever.

The system fit into my comfort zone as most experts agree that investing in lower P/E companies exposes the investor to substantially less risk.

The methodology benefits the small individual investor. Mutual funds, pension, and other institutional investors have too much money to invest in these small companies. The strategy is briefly summarized as Small Cap Value. There are mutual funds that advertise Small Cap Value Funds, but these funds usually require a market capitalization of $1.5

billion to be included. The small individual investor has a great advantage in this area.

"Uncle Dom, is this the only system that will make us millionaires like you?"

"Of course not. Applying a logical systematic system to investing over the years will make you rich. This system made me richer quicker than the strategies recommended to me by the so called pros."

CHAPTER 12

BALANCE SHEETS FOR ENGLISH LIT MAJORS

I am not making fun of English Lit majors, but I am aware that math and numbers make a lot of people nervous and upset. They mistakenly believe that this is something beyond their understanding or comprehension. Take a little bit of time to learn about the numbers and your trip to Richville will be a lot quicker and easier.

Each and every company you could buy a share of stock in is required to file an annual report with the Security and Exchange Commission (the SEC). Actual investors usually receive a glossy, colorful magazine like volume containing a lot of information. Much of the information is the result of the company's public relations department putting a positive spin on things whether the business is going great guns or south along the porcelain highway.

The **annual report** filed with the SEC is filed electronically and is available to anyone on the internet.

Each annual report contains a **consolidated balance sheet.** Be sure to look at one that has been audited by an outside accounting firm. History teaches us that even a big company like Enron or Tyco can play games with accounting and balance sheets, but an audited balance sheet and other financial documents are the best way to get the "numbers" on a particular company.

Balance sheets and a plethora of other information is found on the internet through **EDGAR.** EDGAR stands for Electronic Gathering Analysis and Retrieval. It is where all companies (even foreign ones) are required to file financial reports and other forms with the SEC.

You may find a site that charges a fee for obtaining this information but the SEC site is free.

Forms 10-K and 10-KSB are required to be filed and these forms contain the financial information you want to examine.

Form 10-K is a comprehensive summary of a company's performance. You will find the company's history, executives pay and other compensation, and audited financial statements.

The Balance Sheet is one of the financial statements. Other statements document income, earnings, and cash flow.

Balance means equal or symmetrical. One side equals the other. (As most balance sheets are written the top part equals the bottom part).

Assets

The first side or top of the balance sheet lists the assets. An asset has a positive monetary value. Cash is dollars. Money in the bank. A cash equivalent is something that can readily be converted into cash. A publically traded share of stock is an example of a cash equivalent. A receivable is money that is owed to you. Inventory is the goods you have on hand, often the products that the company has for sale.

Current assets are cash and other assets that can be converted into cash within one year. Another type of current asset is prepaid expenses. This is an asset that cannot be converted into cash. Generally these are bills that have been paid for services or products that have not yet been provided. An example would be a company's supplier delivers defective merchandise and the company gets a credit toward future merchandise.

Non current assets have a conversion into cash with a time frame of more than one year. Non current assets usually include land, buildings, equipment, and fixtures. Other assets that are more difficult to put a dollar figure on are the company's reputation or good will, patents, trademarks, copyrights, and proprietary formulas.

Assets other than cash lose value over time. This loss of value is referred to as **depreciation** or sometimes **amortization**. This is shown as a minus or negative on the separate line of a balance sheet. A minus or negative is a number contained within parentheses (123etc).

Liabilities

A liability is any financial obligation owed by a company. Salaries and benefits such as **pension plans**, or **accounts payable**, and **loans** and **interest on loans** are liabilities.

The time frame of a liability is also measured by the year. Short term debt is due within the year. Long term debt is due more than a year away. There are four main categories of current liabilities.

1. **Accounts payable** is the money the company owes to its suppliers and employees. These are the basic costs of doing business that are owed.
2. **Accrued expenses** are bills the company owes but has not yet paid. Generally they are expenses that are paid on a schedule and the due date has not yet arrived.
2a. A specific accrued expense listed separately is **Income Tax Payable**. These are also bills paid on a schedule and the due date has not yet arrived.
3. **Short term debt** or **notes payable** is debt that has to paid within the year.
4. **Long term debt** is also listed but usually only the amount due within a year as this is a portion of current liabilities.

Equity

On the balance sheet **equity** or **stockholder's equity** is the amount of funds contributed by the stockholders plus the retained earnings or losses of the company.

Retained earnings are the percentage of earnings not paid out as dividends to the stockholders. This is the money the company can reinvest in its business, hopefully to make it grow or to pay off debt.

With this information and a simple calculator it is easy to figure out ratios that are helpful in making an investment choice. Some companies even list some or all of these ratios in their 10-K.

Ratios

Current ratio is a measure of a company's liquidity. Current ratio equals Current Assets divided by Current Liabilities. A company with fewer assets than liabilities is technically bankrupt, therefore you should expect to see a ratio greater than one.

Is higher better? Unfortunately the answer is not necessarily so. If the Current Ratio is too high those assets may suggest that the company is sitting on them rather than using them to make the company grow.

Inventories as an asset may be misleading especially in the retail industry. Going out of business sales, end of season sales, we bought too much of the latest fad that did not catch on sale, can severely slash the true value of the inventory.

Look to **Quick Ratio** to take this problem into consideration. The **Quick Ratio** is Current Assets minus Inventories divided by Current Liabilities.

The **Working Capital to Market Capitalization Ratio** is another device that will help you make sound investment decisions.

Working Capital equals Current Assets minus Current Liabilities. The higher the working capital the more money the company has to spend on growing its business and increasing shareholder (your) value.

Market Capitalization is Shares Outstanding multiplied by the Price per Share added to the Company's Debt. Included in debt is any Preferred Shares the company may have issued.

The formula looks like this:

$$\frac{\text{Working Capital}}{\text{Market Capital}} = \frac{\text{Current Assets - Current Liabilities}}{\text{Shares Outstanding x Price + Debt}}$$

Preferred Stock is sort of a hybrid between a stock and a bond. A preferred share of stock usually has no voting rights attached to it, and it will usually be paid a dividend before a common share. Should the company be liquidated the preferred stockholders will be paid before the common stockholders. Because it is a less risky investment its potential for an increase in value is much less than the common share.

A final helpful ratio is the **Price to Sales Ratio** or **PSR.** It is simply the company's Share Price (Price per Share) divided by the company's **Revenues or Earnings per Share.**

This ratio ignores expenses and debt but because you will be using it to compare companies within the same industry it is a useful calculation to make. The general rule is the lower the ratio the better.

Now armed with this financial information take the plunge. Pick a company and buy the stock.

This is one area the individual investor has a huge advantage over wall street, mutual funds, and all the Pros from Dover. They simply cannot afford to study these companies and buy their shares.

It seems a contradiction that a big firm with billions of dollars cannot afford to invest in a company Rich Uncle Dom or any other investor can afford to buy, but it is absolutely true.

These giants have so much money to invest they would have to buy a majority of shares in these companies to fit them in their portfolios. They would therefore "own" the company and be forced to manage it which is not their business. A **Small Cap** company to them has a minimum market capitalization of $1.5 billion or more.

This is our advantage. This is the area where the small investor will always beat the pros, because it is a field the big guys cannot even get into. Use it to get rich.

CHAPTER 13

SURESLEEP

After the last two chapters your brain might need a rest. The areas of stock picking and reading a balance sheet are mathematical and technical. With a little study it will become second nature to you.

When asked, more than fifty percent of the population claims to have one or more sleep problems. So mathematically that means normal sleep is a problem.

Sleep is a natural suspension of consciousness. The most important word in that definition is natural. Sleep induced by medication should be avoided.

There are supposedly no hard and fast rules about how much sleep a person needs, yet controlled studies conclude that less than seven hours a night leads to poor performance at every level of mental and motor abilities. To acquire great wealth it is necessary to operate at peak performance and proper sleep is necessary to achieve this.

Too little sleep causes a myriad of problems. It could even kill you. Think about you or the guy in the other car falling asleep at the wheel. It's scary.

Proper sleep makes you happier and healthier. Something so important needs to be treated as a skill or ability that needs to be achieved, rather than something that takes care of itself.

Worry and guilt are sleep thieves. Anyone going to bed with worry or guilt will be robbed of restful sleep.

It is easy to intellectualize worry and guilt away. Worrying about a problem does nothing to solve it. Feeling guilty about the past act does nothing to change it. Yet our feelings of guilt and worry persist.

Strong positive emotions can also cause lack of sleep, but this is less problematical. A child unable to sleep on Christmas Eve can wake up to the happiest day of his year. A young woman barely sleeps the night before her wedding, awakes at dawn and is still dancing at midnight.

Be aware of sleep robbers and employ an artificial technique to get the sleep you deserve.

Try not to worry about sleep. A good night of sleep is usually interrupted by periods of wakefulness. Most of these periods of wakefulness are not remembered, but if experienced be aware that this is normal and a good thing, and not something to be worried about.

To sleep you need a comfortable, disturbance free environment. Bed, pillows, and blankets should not be taken for granted. The maximum number of pillows under your head is two. One is OK, more than two is not. If you want to surround yourself with pillows, do so, just no more than two under your head.

Your mattress should be firm and comfortable. A good one will last ten years. Most people feel foolish trying out mattresses in a store and simply lying on one for a moment or two will not tell you much anyway. Do some research and make an informed decision. It is the best any of us can do.

"Uncle Dom, peak performance or not, is sleep going to make me a million dollars?"

"In and of itself, of course not. Proper sleep will make you healthier, more attentive, and enable you to get more done than Josie Sleepyhead."

Hindsight is twenty twenty. Looking back at how I acquired financial riches convinced me that factors not directly connected to finances were as important if not more so than the factors directly related to the money. Remember, I made many failed investment decisions and still made millions. Sleep is very important and so are the other so called non financial factors.

Perhaps an old story illustrates this best.

One day the parts of the body began arguing about which part was the most important. The eyes said they were the most important. Without us the body would not know where to go or how to get there.

We are the most important announced the legs and feet. Without us the body would not be able to go anywhere.

We are the most important claimed the arms and hands. Without us the body would not be able to do anything wherever it went.

I am the most important claimed the butt hole.

With this announcement all the other body parts started laughing. This upset the butt hole and he stopped functioning.

Soon the eyes were not seeing well. Vision was blurry. The feet and legs could not move the body without staggering. The hands began to shake. The body started to die.

All the body parts pleaded with the butt hole to function again. They agreed he was important. Just as important as any of them. So the little butt hole started working again. Soon the legs and feet could move without staggering; the eyes cleared, and the hands stopped shaking. The body functioned smoothly again.

Your sleep schedule is important. Our economy has moved from industrial to service oriented. Shift workers are a small minority of our working population. Many studies of shift workers proved these people had the most sleep problems and that these problems led to significant health problems.

Keep to a schedule. Go to bed the same time every night and get up the same time every morning. If your day includes proper nutrition and sufficient exercise, keeping to your schedule will be a cinch.

Avoid weekend warrior status. Staying up all night Saturday and sleeping through Sunday throws course sand into your sleep engine.

Most researchers tell us not to use the bedroom for any purpose other than sleeping. They counsel against reading or watching television. (Most of them say nothing about sex so I can only conclude they have a much wilder sex life than most of us.)

Reading in bed or watching television will not significantly interfere with your sleep so long as you keep to your sleep schedule. Turn out the light or the TV every night at the same time and there will be no problem. If you often fall asleep with the light or the TV on before your scheduled time, hook the appliances up to a timer so they go off automatically.

The sleep environment should be restful. If total silence is not possible there is nothing wrong with relaxing music from a CD or tape or calming white noise such as waterfalls or waves breaking on a beach.

If you choose music or white noise, play the same thing every night. This triggers the sleep response in you body that now is the time to shut down.

You may employ an artificial method for inducing sleep that is both natural and restful.

Simply begin a mental dialogue with your body starting with your feet and working up to your head.

Mentally say, "My left foot is heavy and is becoming re-laxed, tired and ready for sleep."

If thought diversions interrupt your internal dialogue, do not fight them and do not become angry with yourself or frustrated. Simply continue going through the ritual from where you were interrupted. "My left shoulder is becoming relaxed, tired, and ready for sleep.

Enjoy your night's rest. One of the greatest sleep problems is the mistaken belief that you have a problem. Natural sleep is interrupted by periods of wakefulness. Do not allow these natural occurrences to cause you worry or distress. If you become aware of these waking periods you will be more likely to remember your dreams.

"Uncle Dom, is sleeping really going to make me rich?"

"Absolutely. All of our lessons are important to making a fortune."

CHAPTER 14

WHEN TO SELL

You have done your research and you have purchased shares in the perfect small cap value companies that will skyrocket you to wealth. Glance at the company's numbers every other month or so and watch your bottom line soar. (Wishful thinking. Seriously, I review my investments no more than twice a year.)

You may surprise yourself. Some of your investments may actually achieve such a result.

You have invested your time, effort, and money into choosing an investment. You have researched the company, its management, and the fundamentals. You may have even developed a bit of an emotional attachment to a company. If its price dips, you do not sell. If its price flops, you do not sell. If its price plummets lower than whale droppings, you do not sell.

This is one of your babies. You do not turn your back on one of your children just for a little misbehavior.

If this is your attitude and thinking, beware of the Nigerian who needs a little help getting his fabulous fortune into the U.S. Your money will join the Caribbean monk seal, the Guam flying fox, the pig-footed Bandicoot, and the Dodo bird; something remembered, but no longer in existence.

You used your intelligence and knowledge to make your investments. You must use the same when deciding to sell.

Each investment need only be reviewed twice a year. One of these times should be before your end of year tax return needs to be prepared. Give yourself the time necessary to do something to effect that return in such a way to benefit you. The other should be about six months prior to that time, but the timing of that review is not as critical.

There are six reasons for selling a stock.

1. Mistakes made when buying.
2. Stock is hot.
3. Stock is cold.
4. Change in fundamentals.
5. Balance the portfolio.
6. You need the money.

On occasion you might discover a **mistake** you made in coming to a decision to buy a stock. You may have over-looked an important fact that comes to your attention after you have already made the purchase.

The numbers were right, but you were unaware the president, CEO, and CFO had just been indicted for stock fraud. Take another look. My reasoning might be: Great! Buy some more. The information was out there and the numbers are still O.K.

You may learn your company's business is too dependent on another company. You found the perfect small service company in the financial sector. It provides benefit and retirement packages to other companies. You discover that more than 85% of its sales is to Wal-Mart. Rethink that investment

The second reason to sell is when the **stock is hot**. If the price is climbing to the stratosphere, it is probably no longer a value company. If the P/E ratio widens dramatically rethink the investment. Your research may uncover the fact that the FDA just approved a procedure discovered by the company's stem cell research division that may cure cancer. You could hold on for the ride of a lifetime, or be conservative by selling enough of the stock to recoup your investment and holding the other shares and see what happens.

The **stock is cold**. The stock price starts going south. You discover the fundamentals are the same, and the P/E is dramatically lower. You decide to buy more. Good decision. However if the price has declined and there is no longer a positive P/E run from that dog faster than from Cujo.

Balance the portfolio. You examine your investments as a whole and discover that market changes have caused your portfolio to be too heavily invested in one industry or sector. Personally, when I see my own portfolio in such a state I look for additional investments in other industries and sectors. Keep Paying the Piper.

Selling based on a **change of fundamentals** overlaps the reasons discussed so far. Changes in the numbers, profits, sales, P/E, etc. are changes in fundamentals. Also look for other changes. A significant increase in debt, for example, may not be a bad thing. The company has made a loan to buy up a competitor. Might be a good thing. You examine the competitor and find out its losing money. Maybe not such a good thing. It's losing money, but the owners are pulling huge salaries and not doing much of the work. Back to a good thing. Use the information and make a decision. In the long run you will make a lot of money.

Perhaps you learn that in a family run company the President and CEO is retiring and moving to Tahiti with her twenty-five year old boyfriend and is turning the reins over to her beer swilling son. I would say that is a sell sign.

Real life examples of fundamental changes are usually more subtle. When discovered, examine the information in order to make an informed decision.

Remember these companies are too small to be scrutinized by the so called pros. Your insight and knowledge are very significant. The only thing that should never under any circumstances be sold short is your faith in your ability to make yourself rich.

The final reason for selling a stock is you **need the money**. Be very wary of this reason. Think and rethink your so called need for the money before selling an investment.

If the money is just for stuff, hold off. Instead make partial payments to yourself from your regular earnings until you have saved enough for the purchase, and if you still "need" the money, go for it and make the purchase.

A more legitimate reason for selling is because you need the money for another investment that will grow your wealth indirectly. An example might be the cost of enrolling in a course of study necessary for a pay raise or promotion. Before making the expenditure negotiate with your boss. The company may be willing to contribute or even pay for the whole course.

We may delude ourselves into thinking we "need" things. Selling a stock to invest in a better one is a necessary step in wealth accumulation. Selling a stock for a long weekend trip to a tropical beach may be enjoyable, but thinking it necessary is a financially fatal mistake, because then other things become necessary and block your path to wealth.

"Uncle Dom, did you ever not sell a stock you should have?"

"Many times, nephew. When an investment should have been sold for legitimate reasons I often held onto to it until I found another to replace it. But even with many mistakes, this system made me rich."

CHAPTER 15

HOW MANY HOURS IN YOUR DAY?

Each of us starts out the day with the same twenty four hours. Most of us struggle through with the "same ole same ole" and accomplish little. Then there are some of us with no more ability or even less than average ability who get a lot done, accomplish much, and are a lot happier for their efforts.

A former president of Yale University was asked about the students he prized the most. He praised the "A" students because he found that often these people wrote wonderful books and contributed to man's sum of knowledge. His most prized students, however, were the "C" students who had to work hard to get through the University. This hard work often led these students to great wealth and they contributed significantly to the University's endowment.

There is no need for brilliance to accomplish much and to accumulate wealth.

There is no need for brilliance to accomplish much and to accumulate wealth.

I found it necessary to control my life by controlling my time. Until I graduated from high school my time was pretty much regimented by the school clock. From nine to three I was in school. Travel time, a little home work and some TV and the day was over.

College was a great awakening. Even with a heavy course load of eighteen credits a semester no one stood over you to make sure you did anything. You could find a party, a card game, a bull session, or a beer keg seven nights a week. I quickly realized the evenings' temptations would keep me from the books on a regular basis.

My solution was to structure the days. Between classes was the time I used to read the books, do the assignments, and write the papers. I found a small desk in the math library near my dorm on a floor not accessible by elevator that became my work station.

I wrote my daily schedule down in my notebook. Even though it was more or less the same every week, that habit of writing down a daily schedule is one of the main reasons I am "Rich Uncle Dom" and not just Uncle Dom.

This schedule allowed me to enjoy the evenings and weekends without worrying about the school work not getting done.

The best way to control your life is by controlling your time. There are a lot of neat electronic gadgets you can use to punch in tasks and to tabulate short term and long term goals. My favorite is still pen and notebook. I always have at least three calendars, plus two notebooks. Two of the calendars and one of the notebooks relate to my job and the others allow me to focus on the other aspects of my life.

Focus and write down both long term and short term goals. A goal is specific. It is not a mere hope or dream.

"I want to be rich," is a dream; a hope.

"I will have a million dollar portfolio in twenty years by investing at least ten percent of my earnings in under valued small cap corporations and mutual funds," is a goal.

The achievement of any significant goal requires you to leave your comfort zone. You know what your comfort zone is. It is what you do every day. It is your rut. It is what you go about doing with minimum effort and thought.

One easy method to open yourself to the power of achievement is to simply schedule activities that are unique to you.

Love science fiction? Great. Heinlein, Clarke, Tolkien, Norton, Herbert, and Asimov are some favorite acquaintances I have never met. Continue to read them, but schedule a time each day to read about architecture or opera. The what is not as important as the doing of something different.

Divide your long term goals into general categories significant to your personal life. My general goals were, and still are: Health, Wealth, and Happiness.

When I was a kid I played the board game "Careers." The object was to acquire a sufficient amount of "money, fame, and happiness" toward winning the game. I never had the desire to be famous so I switched health for fame. Use these as yours or try some others such as Career, Wisdom, Talent, Retirement, Family, Fun, Education, Wellness, or Friendship.

Spend some time thinking about what is important to you and write it down. I have been amazed over the years at the power of simply writing words on paper. Thoughts get turned into the action of writing and the writing turns into other actions that ultimately yield the achievement of your aims.

Break down your long term goals into shorter action steps. Your long term goal is to be a millionaire by your thirtieth birthday. You have a high school diploma, you deliver pizza, and you have never earned more than a thousand dollars a week in your life.

Your goal may seem like an impossible dream, but if you write down your action steps on paper and begin to accomplish these small goals you will accomplish what you want to achieve.

Be as specific as possible with long term goals. For example, "I will be a millionaire by my thirtieth birthday by owning and managing my own pizza restaurants in Maryland that sell better tasting pizzas."

It is necessary that your short term goals be as specific as possible. "I will sample different pizzas and talk to people about their favorite pizzas."

"I will work part time in the restaurant that makes the best pizza while I am attending community college learning how to manage a restaurant business."

"I will read one book a month and three articles about the restaurant business."

Write down in your daily schedule the times when you will take these action steps:

Monday.
6:30 a.m. two mile walk. S, shower, and shave. Breakfast of cereal, skim milk, and a banana.
9:00 a.m. Go to library, find a list of books on starting and managing your own restaurant business. Skim through three and choose one that looks good. Read first chapter.

Map out your day writing down the specific action steps that will lead you to achieving your goals. Spend some time each evening or morning actually writing down what you are going to do, keeping in mind that you do not want to keep up the "same ole, same ole" as this puts you in a rut. Remember, get out of your comfort zone to accomplish anything worthwhile.

"Uncle Dom, are you telling us the pizza business will make us rich?"

"Absolutely. Follow these simple lessons and any business, profession, or career will make you rich. Guaranteed."

CHAPTER 16

OMNES VIAE ROMAN DUCUNT
ALL ROADS LEAD TO ROME

My path to extraordinary wealth succeeded by following these simple lessons and investing my "Piper Payments" into small companies my research told me were cheap to invest in, namely small cap value stocks.

You may not feel comfortable with that approach or may not feel you have the ability to pick good companies. You have the ability, trust me, but many investment paths will lead you to great wealth.

Many paths lead to financial freedom. Provided you "Pay the Piper" and "Don't Buy the Second Toaster" and follow the other simple lessons here money will not be one of your worries.

A potential path to explore is mutual funds. A mutual fund is generally a company without fixed capitalization that sells its own shares and uses the pooled capital of its shareholders to invest in a variety of securities of other companies. In short you put up a small amount of money to own a very small percentage ownership of many companies.

There are more mutual funds than the number of individual companies listed on the New York Stock Exchange. Funds are usually designated by the criteria used to choose the companies' shares that will be put in the fund's portfolio. Growth, value, small cap, mid cap, international, large cap, combinations of these, and others are some of the types of funds available for purchase. There are some funds that place morality into the criteria, refusing to buy shares of a company involved in the sale or manufacture of alcohol or tobacco products for one example. Some funds invest in only certain areas of the economy like technology or transportation. Others seek to match common indexes such as the Dow Jones Industrials, the S&P 500, or the Wilshire 5000.

Imagine any criteria and there is a strong likelihood that there is a fund that will match it.

The basic theory of mutual fund investing is that there is safety in diversity. Your eggs are never in one basket. The fund can afford to buy shares in many more companies than you could invest in on you own. You are therefore saved from a financial catastrophe of the collapse of a single company that makes up a large percentage of your portfolio. Think Enron and the huge number of its employees whose life savings were wiped out when the company went down the tubes.

Be aware if most of your investment is in a single fund that emphasizes only one area of the economy, energy, for example. Your entire savings will rise and fall with that part of the economy.

If you Google mutual funds you will find more than 100,000,000 sites to look at. That is a pretty daunting task.

You may want to limit your search into one or two of the large families of mutual funds such as T. Rowe Price, Fidelity, or Vanguard. Each of these and fund groups like them offer a wide spectrum of investment choices. You will be able to find an investment approach you are comfortable with.

Be always aware of the costs that are added to your investment dollars. At one time most funds carried a load, or sales charge. Every time you bought or sold you were charged a fee. Now no-load funds predominate, but be aware of the expenses each one charges. These charges are easy to find. Do not ignore them and not think small numbers are insignificant. One half of one percent over the life of your investment could cost more than a new car.

Assume two funds with an expense difference of 1%. A ten thousand dollar investment in the cheaper, with five thousand dollars ($5000.000) a year in additional investments and an annual return of only 8% would make you an additional $30,000.00 in twenty years over the investment that only cost you an additional 1%.

As a rule index funds have the cheapest expenses. An index fund simply needs to mirror the index it represents. No expert needs to be hired or paid to pick stocks or research companies.

One method many feel comfortable with is to invest in two index funds. One that mirrors the entire economy, and the other a conservative bond fund that pays consistent dividends. You invest most of your money in the stock fund, especially when you are years from retirement, then gradually increase your contribution to the bond fund. There are even funds that take a similar approach and do this for you. The Vanguard Target Retirement Funds are but just one example.

You may conclude that since small cap value worked for me all you need to do is to invest in a small cap value index fund. This is not a bad idea, but keep in mind that these mutual funds have so much money to invest that it is almost impossible for them to buy shares in a truly small company. These funds invest in "small companies" with a minimum capitalization of nearly two billion dollars ($2,000,000,000.00)

Do not try to time your investments. Bad news has always been a signal for me to look around for some investment opportunity, but if you've paid the piper and have the money to invest, take the plunge. Keep in mind that if you are looking to invest there is always one or more segments of the economic environment that are going through a tough patch. It takes a little courage but the rewards are worth it.

Dollar Cost Averaging is a theory that says put the same amount into your investment at evenly scheduled periods of time. For example invest one thousand dollars ($1000.00) per month each and every month. The theory is that you are buying both the highs and lows. If you are lucky enough to have twelve thousand dollars ($12000.00) to invest, I say do it right away. There is little sense parking that money in some minimal return account just so you can dollar cost average.

A True Tale

The measure of a mutual fund manager or stock picker is to meet or beat the return of the S&P 500 Stock Index.

The S&P 500 is an index containing the stocks of 500 Large Cap Corporations. Most of these companies are American and many are household names such as Microsoft and Coca Cola. The index is the most notable of the many indices. It is owned and maintained by Standard & Poor, a division of McGraw-Hill.

Legg Mason, Inc. is a global asset management firm headquartered in Baltimore, Maryland. It has assets totaling over $1 trillion.

In investment circles it had a famous mutual fund and a superstar manager. The fund is the Legg Mason Value Trust and the manager was Bill Miller. Bill Miller is the Tiger Woods and Peyton Manning of the investment world. The fund is a multicap fund, investing in stocks of mixed capitalization.

The fund and the manager are famous because of the "streak". For a fifteen year period ending in 2006 Bill Miller and the Legg Mason Value Trust beat the S&P 500. This was an unheard of record, making financial headlines worldwide and making Bill Miller a very wealthy man. It is a record, they say, which will never be broken. (They also said that about Babe Ruth and home runs.)

The point of this true tale is that anyone who simply invested in an S&P 500 index fund for the same period would have done better than almost every single investment professional in the industry. These are folks who drive BMWs and live in mansions. Yet anyone who followed a simple low cost investment strategy of investing in such an index would be a financial superstar up there close to Bill Miller.

There are many roads to extraordinary wealth. Hop on any one and you will get there.

"So Uncle Dom, are you saying ignore your system of small cap value and just dump it into an S&P Index fund?"

"No. I became wealthy from the lessons I learned while I was putting my money where my mouth is and not just to kiss it goodbye.

"I made many mistakes. These are the lessons that work. If you choose not to make the effort, by all means go the simple route. You will not get as rich, perhaps but you will do very well."

They say money can't buy you happiness, but wouldn't you want the chance to find out for yourself?

CHAPTER 17

SORRY, ANOTHER MATH LESSON

You may think putting your money into an index fund and doing nothing else is the way you should go. You may be sold on its simplicity and their claim that everything is done for you. You will be sent a lot of paper and you will get an end of year statement, but be sure to keep some simple records of your own. You will put thousands extra in your pocket.

It is necessary at the very least to make a record of the dividends and capital gains you have earned and paid taxes on over the years. You should also keep a record of the dates of purchase, the purchase price, and the number of shares purchased. This is known as your cost basis. This will make a significant difference in the money you keep in you pockets when you sell this fund or transfer the assets.

A simple example illustrates the concept. You spend one thousand dollars ($1000.00) for a fund. Your end of year statement shows the value of the fund when your bought it, its value now and the dividends and gains you reinvested into the fund. These figures give you some taxable income you must pay taxes on that year if the fund is not part of a retirement account. Even if part of your retirement the tax man will eventually come calling.

Years go by. You have automatically reinvested all dividends and capital gains and your fund is now worth three thousand dollars ($3000.00) and you decide to cash out and reinvest elsewhere. If you have not done some very simple record keeping you owe Uncle Sam on the difference between one thousand and three thousand. If you have kept simple records you can deduct the amounts of dividends and gains you have already paid taxes on. You can also factor in the purchase price of the shares your reinvested dividends and gains bought. If the fund has gone up in value your purchase price on these additional shares may be more, so your gain is less, and your taxes are less. Even though the fund tries to keep its own purchase price at about a dollar a share keeping track of these numbers pays off. Paying only what you owe to your other Uncle, Sam, is a blessing and a duty we all have.

There are about thirty lines on the average sheet of looseleaf paper. So a single piece of paper (front and back) is enough paper to keep thirty to sixty years worth of simple records for a mutual fund or stock.

Put the name of the stock or the fund and its symbol at the top of the page then use a line to write in your yearly gains, losses and dividends. The sophisticated investor makes a note of the number of shares purchased each month from the reinvested dividends and gains.

CHAPTER 18

WE'RE THE PROS FROM DOVER

This expression may originate from the 1968 book M*A*S*H by Richard Hooker.

Hawkeye explains how he would walk into a pro shop at a golf course, introduce himself with a phony name and claim he was the pro from Dover. He claimed he would get to play golf for free eight out of ten times.

The expression means an outside expert or consultant.

Another origin might be a reference to the English port of Dover and the pros, i.e. prostitutes there. In any event:

In the movie he's in a Korean hospital with Trapper John and they are the Pros from Dover, there to crack open some kid's chest.

After my initial investment into stocks I began to develop the system that worked so well for me, investing in very small cap value companies. Years later when I realized a significant part of my entire financial worth was in these companies few people had even heard of, I got scared.

I doubted myself. I called on the "Pros from Dover", stock brokers and financial planners.

Biggest financial mistake I ever made. Thankfully, I only turned over about half my assets to them. I assumed they would do better than me because I was self taught and realized I was focusing on a very limited and specific part of the investment landscape.

I did not let them control all my investments only because I liked looking for these no name companies and learning about their business and the people who ran them and worked for them. Putting my money on them was exciting. It was never a horse race because my goals were long range. I could have invested in these companies through the Pros, but I learned quickly that the Pros had other ideas for my money.

I believed then as I do now that if you take the time, effort, and expense to hire an expert, it is foolish not to follow his advice. If your gut gives you a different message go get a second or even a third opinion from another expert or two.

If you will never feel comfortable investing on your own and need help from a Pro lean from my mistakes and get the right Pro.

You want a Pro that is going to maximize your returns and minimize your risks. Keep in mind that these two goals are usually mutually exclusive. More risk means more gain or loss. Less risk means less gain or loss. You may want a Pro that is going to decide everything in your financial life, or one that is going to be involved in one specific part only.

Your first step is to decide what you want the Pro doing for you. This will help you focus on your financial goals. Write it down. **Write it down.**

Next, prepare a series of questions you are going to ask the Pro. Do not just go over some things in your mind. Write down specific questions. Have these questions with you when you talk with the Pro and take down notes. Any legitimate Pro will respect your efforts.

Ask about the Pro's background. Where did he go to college? What was his major? Is this his first job? What experience does he have?

Ask about how he is compensated; how he gets paid. Most stock brokers are paid at least in part by commission. This puts a significant conflict of interest between you and your broker. His best interest is to do a lot of buying and selling. Your interest will more often be a buy and hold strategy.

If no commissions are paid to him, how is he getting paid? Does the company have an interest in what he is selling?

How are investment decisions made? What information and materials are relied upon before a recommendation is made?

Have any formal complaints been made against the Pro? What were the results of these complaints? Check the Central Registration Depository (CRD) for the Pro's disciplinary history. Your state's regulator is readily available from the National Association of Securities Dealers, Inc. (NASD).

Get some names and phone numbers of other customers or clients of the Pro. If the information is confidential ask him if he would ask three or four of his clients to call you.

Listen carefully to the questions he asks you. He must ask about your specific goals. Are you looking for a safe and secure road to a comfortable retirement at some definite date in the future? Are you adverse to risk or do you want to put some money aside to gamble on a potential high gain? Do you have other investment assets such as a 401(k) or other retirement benefit with your employer? If so does the employer match any part of your contribution?

If your employer's retirement plan allows a number of sensible options for investing the Pro should advise you to maximize your investment there before turning to his products, services, or buy recommendations.

The Pro needs to ask you about your family and expenses. Are there children who need college to be paid for? Are you aware of any major expense that you must pay in the near future?

Remember it is your money. Do not be embarrassed to ask these and other questions that you have thought about and written down. And written down. **And written down.**

CHAPTER 19

IT'S JUST STUFF

Bumper sticker: The person who dies with the most stuff wins.
Did you hear that Mattel came out with a new Barbie? Divorcee Barbie. She comes with all of Ken's stuff.

During a life time people accumulate a variety of things. If we think of all these things simply as stuff we will go a long way to minimize the number and cost of these possessions.

One of Webster's definition for stuff is "worthless objects." If you spell it stuf it's a four letter word beginning with s. Another four letter word beginning with s is sh*t.

The basic human needs are food, clothing , and shelter. In this modern world most of us would have to add to the necessity list, things such as education, communication, and transportation. After the basics, the rest is just stuff.

Anyone who has lived through a devastating tornado, hurricane, or other natural disaster will tell you how happy they are to be alive. For the most part what they lost is just stuff. If asked if only one thing could be replaced that thing is usually something of minimum monetary value such as a photo album or some simple object a young son or daughter made for them.

I am not suggesting material things are not worth having. We all work long and hard and are entitled to enjoy the rewards of our labors, but keep in mind that many purchases are spur of the moment and give us no real value or lasting pleasure.

Pause before making a purchase, especially an expensive one. Analyze whether the purchase will significantly improve you or your family's quality of life.

Another measure of value will be you calculation of the stuff's value a year or two in the future. Do not think you may only purchase an asset with an appreciation factor, but ask yourself if a year from now this thing will have added to you or your family's happiness or well being.

Is the stuff you are buying complete or are there other expenses involved? Many of us can remember a disappointing present or toy because Santa forgot the batteries.

King Gillette became a very rich man by basically giving razors away and charging for the blades that had to be replaced constantly.

The more expensive the stuff you buy, the greater the additional expenses normally accrue. Buying a big SUV without thinking about the price of gas, service, maintenance, and insurance is being short sighted at best.

If you make a decision to buy some stuff be sure to do some comparative shopping. When doing so compare apples with apples. So many things have slight variances that affect price. The best method is to compare by the exact same model number.

Many people go to enormous lengths to comparison shop for minor, less expensive things, but make quick decisions about the more expensive; often simply by relying on someone else's opinion.

When I look at companies to invest in I know I am going to do twelve to twenty four hours of research and study at a minimum before coming to a decision to buy or not. All major purchases should be studied as carefully.

Become aware of the pitfalls of instant gratification. This world offers an enormous variety of stuff available at our fingertips. Infomercials offer us stuff that will greatly improve our lives at little cost, little effort, and only a free phone call away. Do not be a sucker. Keep your money for something you believe in, something you are confident will make you happy or improve the quality of your life.

Never compound the problem by purchasing your stuff on credit. This is financial seppuku (hara kiri, ritualistic suicide).

Some go so far overboard that after buying too much stuff they have to rent a storage vault to keep it in. Once each month you pay to keep this stuff you can only visit. Absurd.

It is hard to earn and keep some money, but it is relatively easy to put that money to work for you. When money goes to work it works twenty four hours a day, seven days a week. It never takes a vacation, goes on strike, or gets sick. It is obvious. Money can be your greatest employee.

CHAPTER 20

QUALITY OF LIFE POINTS

Years ago I realized I was a millionaire. That was a nice feeling. It was pretty amazing to me that living an ordinary life could accomplish what I had always believed to be an extraordinary feat.

Any euphoria I felt lasted less than a day. Telling the world about this accomplishment would only be bragging and the hassles of fending off strangers with their hands out would not be worth my time. It would be even a greater hassle to deal with friends with their hands out.

If it was not for the need I felt to explain to the young ones in my extended family that becoming rich was something they could all accomplish by following the simple to understand rules I learned on my own journey, this would not have been written.

Becoming a millionaire made me think about what to do with some of that money. The amazing conclusion I came to was to do absolutely nothing. There were no significant purchases that would make me happier, laugh more, get healthier, reduce stress, or greatly improve my "Quality of Life".

All of us should spend a few moments each day to determine what is important in our lives. Following these money rules will eliminate or, at least, significantly reduce money worries, but that is only one aspect of life.

Concentrate on what is truly important.

Health is something we need to work on every day. Even the healthiest of us can and will succumb to accidents or disease that will detract from our Quality of Life. Do not focus on what might happen and what we have no control over rather focus on what you do have control over. Maintain the healthy diet your grandmother taught you. Exercise or play physically every day. The endorphins secreted by your brain will put a smile on your face.

Go out of your way to put yourself in circumstances that will give you more laughter and joy. Watch a musical comedy. Volunteer to chaperone children at play. Learn how to tell a good joke and be sure to tell one every day. Associate with happy groups or with people who are doing good works. The feeling of satisfaction and well being will be immense.

Get out of your comfort zone and do something for fun that is not what you are used to. Learn to scuba dive and vacation to warm water destinations. Try square or ballroom dancing or both. Go out for a church choir or try out for a part in community theater. As long as you can laugh at yourself and not take yourself too seriously you will have a ball. Sure, there is always nervous energy when you do something new or different, but the rewards are extraordinary.

Be aware of the stress factors and do your best to reduce or eliminate the stress. Some times all you need to do is be aware that something is causing you stress and that your stress reaction is normal and ordinary.

Generally all change is stressful, even positive change like a job promotion, a vacation, or marriage.

Major stressors such as divorce, separation, death of a spouse or close family member, personal injury or illness, job loss, criminal prosecution or imprisonment, are difficult to deal with. Family support, someone to talk to or even exercise will help you deal with the stress, but be aware that it is natural and ordinary to feel stress because of changes in your life.

One simple method to reduce the effect of a particular stressor is to simply acknowledge it. Take out your notebook and write down in as few words as possible what your particular stressor is. Then write that your reaction to this is normal and natural and that it will pass; that there are certain steps to take to deal with it or to change the situation. Write down the steps. Take the first step, check it off your list, and go to the second step.

The first time I was assigned a major term paper in college was a significant worry for me. This paper was virtually my whole grade for the course. The few reports I was required to do in high school were only a few pages and only a small amount of research and study was necessary to complete those projects.

This project was the equivalent of a small book. References had to be studied and checked. Quotations and citations were expected. This was before desktop computers and the internet so the dusty shelves of the library would have to be visited on many occasions. I thought this might be the end of college for me.

I got out a notebook. The first thing I wrote on the first page was "Term Paper. Underneath that I wrote, "Don't let this stuff (I did not actually use the word stuff) drive you crazy. Hundreds before you have done it, and hundreds after you will get it done."

I then made a quick list that included topic, references, subjects to be explored in the topic, introduction, body, conclusion, personal opinion?, expert opinion, and will this project help my sex life?

My little joke to myself substantially reduced the stress and my initial list showed me that the project was doable and could be broken down into a finite number of tasks, each of which could be accomplished.

The deadline given by the professor was the last class of the semester. He required nothing before that date. He had given us a page with a list of over one hundred topics and a concluding paragraph that any topic in the field (Sociology) would be equally acceptable.

I knew I had a tendency to put things off to the last minute. This was the biggest project I had ever been assigned. I knew only that the last minute would not give me enough time to get it done.

I wrote down interim deadlines in my notebook. I gave myself to the next class to come up with two topics. Two, because I wanted to check out the library to see which topic had the most available books and other research materials available. I wrote down a deadline for an initial outline, a second outline, and a final outline. I figured if I just kept building on an outline, by the time I got to the writing part most of the work would have already been done. That proved to be the case.

The paper was done on time and I got the highest grade in the class and a personal letter of congratulations from the professor and the Chairman of the Department. (That's a lie, but not a big fat one. I did ace the course).

"Uncle Dom, are you really trying to tell us that it is necessary to take a sociology course and complete a major term paper in order to become millionaires?"

"Of course not."

The skill learned from such an effort is the important lesson. In your job, career, or investment plan, completing large projects is essential.

Every large project seems complicated, overwhelming, and nearly impossible. Stop and think. I always think better with pen and paper. Take the project, break it down into small pieces, set time constraints on the completion of each task and take the first step. Check it off your list and do the next thing.

You can worry all you want about whether you will complete the project to your satisfaction or the satisfaction of your boss or supervisor. But be sure to write down this sentence more than once: "Worry is a waste of time and energy. Worry gets nothing accomplished. I am just going to keep on taking the next step."

Silly? Perhaps. But take the few seconds it takes to write the sentences down and actually take the next step forward. You will be amazed at what you accomplish.

CHAPTER 21

WINDFALLS

Windfalls are unexpected strokes of good luck. Economic windfalls include an unplanned bonus at work, a winning lottery ticket, an inheritance, a stock that soars unexpectedly, a promotion at work, or a cash gift from a relative or friend.

For most people these funds just burn the proverbial hole in the pocket until they are spent. More stuff gets added to the stuff pile. A fleeting whim is stroked. A couple argues about what should be purchased. Worst case: it is used as a down payment on some "unnecessary" purchased on credit.

Wake up. Sniff the java. These sums added to your wealth will grow with you and become a year or more of retirement, a dream vacation, or best of all the elimination of your money concerns.

Every first year psychology student learns that there are two major problems faced by the average couple: money and sex. Worry and stress about money usually leads to the sexual problems. Remember the words of Forrest Gump when he learned he did not have to worry about money anymore: "Good. One less thing."

If you think the sum is too small to make a difference review <u>Time Grows Money</u> and <u>You Can't Afford the Second Toaster.</u> The big numbers for a home or automobile are significant, but tossing away these opportunities is shortsighted in the least and just plain stupid at best.

Create your own windfall. One way to do this is by getting a second job doing something you enjoy, and would even spend money to do. One friend is a baseball fan. Actually more of a fanatic. A season ticket package to his beloved *Baltimore Orioles* costs hundreds of dollars. He is an usher at a box seat section of the stadium. He gets to go to every home game and they pay him for the privilege. Some of the money he earns takes him and his wife on a trip to a World Series game every year. The rest gets put away for retirement.

Many people get the entrepreneurial urge. There is no need to dive into the deep end of the business world, just get your feet wet in the baby pool. Start a sideline or niche business. A colleague of mine retired. He wanted a second career as a public school teacher. He discovered that despite his doctorate degree he was ineligible to teach because he lacked a teaching certificate or education degree. Unwilling to go back to school to do something he viewed as altruistic he began a tutoring program. He began tutoring upper and upper middle class middle and high school students. He now employs fifteen other part time tutors and a full time administrator.

Get paid for your opinions. There's an old expression, "Opinions are like a#@holes. Everybody's got 'em and most of 'em stink." There are research groups throughout this country who will pay you for trying their products and providing some feedback. You might have to travel a few miles but you will get paid. You will not make a lot of money, but the money you make will turn into a lot of money if invested for a number of years.

Sell your stuff. Most of us have many possessions we have no need of, or never use. Get involved in a neighborhood yard sale or advertise in one of the free newspapers or on line. One person's garbage is another's treasure. Take advantage. Clean out a closet, room, or attic and put the money away.

"So, Uncle Dom you are saying that when you croak and leave us all that money, that will be our windfall?"

Your windfall was the miniature golf at the beach and the veggie pizza. Follow these simple rules and make yourselves rich.

CHAPTER 22

IT'S CHEAPER TO BE RICH

America is a great country. Here anyone can become rich. Once you are rich (even just upper middle class), living costs less. It's cheaper to be rich.

If you are rich you can get a checking account with no fees. It even pays a little interest. The poor person is stuck with the account that has fees for everything. Even worse the poor person might be forced to use check cashing services and money orders and pay very high fees. One year's difference is an extra one thousand dollars ($1000.00) in Rich Uncle Dom's pocket.

The rich person puts all his purchases on a no fee credit card, allows the money to grow in a money market fund earning interest until the bill comes due, and then pays off the balance. .

The poor person pays the minimum amount due and is stuck with non-deductible interest that amounts to thousands of dollars over a life time. The rich invest those thousands and get richer. The poor keep paying the high fees and interest rates. Uncle Dom nets an extra one thousand five hundred dollars ($1500.00) each and every year.

The poor person gets a paycheck. He pays taxes on the money he earns. The rich person can defer earnings and realize wealth in the form of capital gains, deferred and retirement income. He then gets taxed at a reduced rate.

Tax reformers yell, "Tax the rich and the big corporations." The reality is that the tax burden falls on the middle class. It has always been this way and it always will. There are a lot of us rich folks around, but if the middle class did not pay the brunt of the tax the government would go bankrupt. These numbers are harder to calculate, but Rich Uncle Dom gets at least another seven hundred fifty dollars ($750.00) extra each and every year.

If the poor person can afford a house, he pays a higher interest rate for a mortgage than the rich person. Usually the poor person will have to buy an older home in an urban area. That urban home is not as energy efficient as the new home in the suburbs, so the poor person pays more for his heating and cooling energy. Add extra mortgage and energy expense and there is Rich Uncle Dom stuffing an extra one thousand two hundred dollars ($1200.00) into his expando wallet.

People who live in urban areas pay more for home and car insurance. The poor person can only afford to pay monthly, therefore his fees and interest are greater than the rich person who pays these bills only once or twice a year.

Most grocery stores in urban areas charge more for food. The Super Wal-Marts and the Uber Food Market are almost non- existent in our cities. So the poor person has to spend more in transportation costs to get to the store or resort to the neighborhood shop that has to charge much more for groceries that often do not include the fresh fruit and vegetables that are such an important part of a healthy life. Perhaps the numbers here are not as significant, but it means that Rich Uncle Dom could eat steak for the cost of the poor person's hamburger.

Mae West said it best: "I've been rich and I've been poor. Believe me, rich is better."

CHAPTER 23

BE HAPPY

DON'T WORRY BE HAPPY-Meher Baba
MONEY CAN'T BUY ME LOVE- Lennon-McCartney

Assuming you have mastered all the necessary lessons for the accumulation of wealth, then that's it. A life of ease and happiness will be yours until you die.

Not quite. Even the big lottery winners return to the same level of happiness they were in before winning the lottery. They returned to their pre lottery feelings of happiness in less than five years. An obsolete definition of happiness was good fortune or prosperity. Now the experts and most of us would accept the modern definition of "a state of well-being and contentment," or "a pleasurable or satisfying experience."

There is an old adage: Money can't buy happiness. That is not necessary true. It has been found time and again that a certain amount of money is necessary for a person to have a chance at happiness. If you do not have enough money for the true necessities of life the stress, frustration, and dread of day to day life keep you from being happy.

Once there is enough for food, clothing, shelter, and transportation the state of happiness becomes a factor of many things, but more money is not one of them.

The purpose of this chapter is to teach you a few things to make the journey through life a pleasant and happy one. Happiness is a state of well being, but it also a goal worth achieving. Like most goals it is easier to achieve with a well thought plan. The best plans in my experience start with a pencil and paper or the electronic gizmo of your choice.

Even though wealth alone will not bring you happiness, acting happy and dealing with others as if you are truly happy will make you wealthier. The person who gets along with others, who is pleasant to be around, who is welcome to play in the sandbox of life at any time is the one who gets the promotion or raise. Money for happiness? Not really. Happiness for money? A reality.

Write down the things that make you happy. Many of us are happy in natural settings of physical beauty. Reading a good book or even one of lesser academic merit with a lot of action and diabolical maiming is enjoyable for us. The movie industry churns out hundreds of films giving pleasure to millions. Achieving a goal or acquiring a new skill is enjoyable.

It is important to keep in mind that it is the journey that should make you happy, and not just the end result. Getting there is the point and not just the getting. Not many of us are destined to be able to hit a major league fastball, but playing a softball game on a summer evening with friends or co-workers can be a lot of fun.

Practice being happy. This may sound silly, but it works. Smile for no reason at all. Pick one day and smile at every one whose path you cross. Some might look away and pretend they did not see you, but most of the folks will smile back. It is a simple exercise that pays dividends and these dividends are free of any taxes or other expenses.

Learn to tell a joke. Telling a good joke or a funny story and getting a good reaction is great, but even the groaner or the flat dud often brings an inward smile to the listener.

Practice being emotionally expressive. Speak slowly, freely, and clearly, pausing for dramatic effect. Be sure to enunciate the punch line clearly.

Choose a story or joke appropriate for the audience. The story of the three salesman and the farmer's daughter might be O.K. at the tavern with some friends, but probably best to be avoided at the ladies sodality.

Avoid racial slurs, hate speech, insults and crude language. There is an audience for that type of material, but since our goal is our own happiness, stick to less offensive material.

Do not take yourself too seriously. There is a time to be serious, but even at the more serious moments a self deprecating remark or gentle jab or poke at yourself makes the most onerous task more pleasant, and the people you are with will enjoy being with you.

Be thankful for what you have. Write down five things you are thankful for. It may be health, a good job, friends, spouse, family, a skill or talent, anything you would miss if you were suddenly without.

Each night in bed before you sleep meditate on these positives of your life. This has a calming effect and helps induce peaceful sleep. Sufficient, restful sleep contributes to wealth accumulation. It also contributes to happiness. The person with insufficient sleep is never as happy as the one with proper rest, assuming other factors are the same.

Being tired leads to stress and crankiness, which leads to weakened effort and inefficiency, which leads to less being accomplished, which leads to less overall enjoyment. The result is less money and less joy and happiness.

If a telemarketer offered you a product guaranteed to make you lose weight, earn more money, make you healthier, and happier, how much would you be willing to pay assuming the claims were true and verifiable? Probably a lot. Proper sleep and rest are free, and study after study prove the accuracy of this claim.

Express gratitude sincerely.

Make eye contact, smile, and say thank you to all the people who do you a small service. This would include a cashier, waitress, bank teller, or the total stranger who holds a door for you. These little courtesies add up and create a feeling of well being. Happiness not only makes you money, it is healthy too. Happiness reduces stress, aids in controlling proper blood pressure, and contributes greatly to those quality of life points we all strive for.

Be sure to send a note of thanks or an email to anyone who has done a special service for you. You might be surprised at how few letters of thanks are sent to the doctors who have saved peoples lives. Sending a thank you card to the mechanic who works on your car will make his day and you can be sure your auto will be cared for, and the price for future services will be fair.

Send a small gift to a friend or family member, but send it anonymously. They may be certain you are the sender, but if asked just smile and say you have no idea where it came from, maybe the Easter Bunny or the Great Pumpkin had something to do with it. The value of the gift is not important. Something expensive is not appropriate for a gesture of this nature and is actually counterproductive.

Spend time with the people you enjoy being around. Actual face to face time is usually more enjoyable, but in the digital world, emails, voice messages, tweets, chats, and the like are more common. Just take a little time to be sincere and transmit something you know the receiver will enjoy. All of us probably have a contact that sends us every piece of garbage he comes across. Don't be that guy.

Just as we should spend as much time as we can with the people we enjoy, minimize your contact with the negative people in your life. If possible avoid such contact altogether. You know who I am talking about. The world is made up of many nay-sayers, complainers, criticizers, put down artists, nit pickers, and just plain jerks. These people offer few if any quality of life points.

You should be aware that certain emotions or feelings are quality of life sappers. These take away from your happiness and consequently your wealth building.

Three of the most common of these are guilt, worry, and resentment. None of these provide any benefit to you and time spent on these emotions is lost and often causes you to spend more wasted time wallowing there.

Guilt is the experience of realizing or believing that the person has violated a moral standard and bears significant responsibility for that violation. Guilt is also the belief that an action or inaction on the part of the person has caused a negative consequence upon that person or another. The guilt exists even if the person has not truly done anything wrong, or has not caused the consequence.

Simply being aware that guilt is a wasted emotion goes a long way in relieving the guilt. Practical methods of eliminating or, at least, minimizing guilt are remorse, atonement, and cognition.

Remorse and atonement often go together. If you feel you have wronged another, make a sincere apology to her. Be prepared with a concrete offer of atonement to make up for your action and not just on open ended offer of "What can I do to make this up to you?"

Cognition is the ability to intellectually remove oneself from the event or emotion and objectively examine the relevant facts. After an objective examination of the facts the conclusion is often that you are not a bad or evil person, or that you are not the true cause of the negative event. If the objective examination leads you to conclude that you do have some responsibility show your remorse and atone.

Worry is concern about some future event. Worry can prevent us from going forward and can take from us the joys and rewards of our efforts.

Some worry might be beneficial. If a person wears a seatbelt and obeys the rules of the road because he is worried about the physical, emotional, and mental trauma that results from an auto accident, that is a good thing,

Much of worry is just a waste. We worry about things that might occur. We worry about things that might not occur. The key word is might. Rather than worry, spend your time and effort to do the things that will assist you in making the things you want to occur to occur, and to make the things you do not want to occur to not occur.

One tool to aid you in placing worry in a proper context is to imagine the worse thing that can happen. It is not an impossible stretch to imagine that the worse case scenario is constant, searing pain, a horrible quality of end of life, and a miserable death. After that conclusion do a mental computation of the odds of that actually happening. End result is always that the worse case scenario is always real bad, but not likely.

Any example of something worrisome can logically lead to this conclusion. For example, you are worried about a promotion at work. You do not get the promotion. This depresses you. You drink too much alcohol because you are feeling low. You drive a car. Accident. Horrible pain. Hospital. Hospice. Death.

A better expenditure of the time spent worrying is to read a book on how to get a promotion at work, ask a boss about what extra work you could perform to earn a promotion, or take a class to learn a necessary skill to make you a better employee.

The third happiness sapper is resentment. Resentment is a feeling of indignant displeasure or persistent ill will at something regarded as a wrong, insult, or injury.

The feeling can be caused by something that actually occurred, or by something you think occurred. The thing that actually occurred may have caused the result or maybe did not. From the analysis we can see that much of resentment is misplaced and just wrong.

Even if the resentment is based on a real assessment of the facts and situation, the resentment we harbor is just another happiness robber.

If you were the victim of harassment, bias, prejudice, injustice, discrimination, physical or emotional abuse, or any unfair treatment it is natural to feel resentment.

Unfortunately, much of resentment is felt toward someone who is supposed to be close to you. A fifty eight year old woman still harbors resentment toward her late mother because she felt Mom treated her sister better. Maybe Mom did treat her sister better. Maybe it was wrong of Mom to treat her sister better. Maybe if Mom had it to do all over again with the benefit of 20-20 hindsight, she would still treat her sister better.

The true sadness of this example is that the resentment cannot be resolved with Mom. Mom is dead. But the resentment can still be resolved or, at least dealt with.

The key to dealing with resentment is communication and forgiveness. The pop psychologists have a rallying phrase: "Get over it."

If your resentment is toward someone you have an ongoing relationship with, it is imperative to deal with the resentment. Continued resentment will poison the relationship and if not resolved will cause significant emotional turmoil and unhappiness to the person who harbors the resentment. This is particularly gruesome if the resentment has been triggered by a real affront or injustice. The person who has been wronged, feels the resentment, and suffers the negative consequences of that resentment.

Attempt to communicate with the person you resent. Calmly state your feelings and why you believe they exist. Avoid accusations and use of the "you" word.

" I feel hurt when I am told I do not do enough to support the family," is a better path to communication and the beginning of the elimination of the resentment, then, "Why don't you shut your mouth about money, and get a job yourself."

The whole psychology of interpersonal communication between spouses and family members fill books that fill libraries or computer discs. Be aware that the resentment you feel hurts you and you are the one best in a position to do something about correcting the situation.

Another method of dealing with resentment is to objectively identify the source of the resentment, be open and aware to the reality that your own life would be better without the feelings of resentment, freely forgive the person who has caused you to feel the resentment, and envision your future free from the feelings and restraints the resentment has caused you.

A final method of dealing with resentment with either a person who is still part of your life or someone who has died is the letter. Compose a letter to the person detailing all the wrongs he committed and all the negative feelings you have suffered and for how long. Write down all the positive and wonderful things that would have occurred in your life without the wrongs done you. Finally tell the person she is unconditionally and without qualification forgiven. Tell her that you are free of the chains that those actions have hung upon you. Reiterate all the wonderful things which will occur in your future because of this new freedom. Finally: Do not send the letter. Do not send the letter. **Do not send the letter.**

Life is more circular than linear. One thing both affects and effects another. Affect because one action influences an outcome. Effect because a certain action brings about a result. Proper sleep aids wealth accumulation, wealth accumulation aids happiness, happiness aids sleep, which aids wealth accumulation. It is a nice circle to be on.

Another significant part of this circle is exercise. Exercise contributes to our monetary bottom line. Exercise contributes a great deal to our happiness account.

You can learn all about endorphins, dopamine, and the like and get an understanding why daily physical activity is such a powerful catalyst to our physical, mental, emotional, and financial well being. Learning the whys often contributes to the doing, but the doing is the key.

Most of these lessons are easy to learn. The hard part is the doing. Write down your goals. Set a reasonable time-table, but one with a challenge. Write down the steps necessary to meet or surpass your goals. Take the first step. **Take the first step.** Then take the next. **Then the next.** Enjoy the journey.

Made in the USA
Lexington, KY
07 September 2014